ARIS

A K-9 Hero's Life
Before, During & After
9/11

Bob Wank

Bob Wank
Lake Forest, CA 92630

Aris A K-9 Hero's Life Before, During & After 9/11/ Bob Wank. -- 1st edition

ISBN 978-1-7356430-2-1
ISBN 978-1-7356430-3-8 E-book
Library of Congress Control Number: 2020918755

Main copy editing by Dan Frio

Cover design by Robyn Do

Interior design by Garrett Wank

Cover photo by Andrea Booher/FEMA News Photo

Rear cover photo by Jerry Manson/OCSD

Printed in the United States of America

For additional information, visit www.bobwank.com

In honor of Aris

and working dogs everywhere

FOREWORD

by Robert Patterson

Chief Fire Officer (retired), National Urban Search and Rescue IST Lead

It was good to hear about Bob's intent to write about his and Aris's time together. Stories of public service, sacrifice, and hard work and perseverance are sometimes lost in the macro. The interesting thing about Bob and Aris's experience is that their involvement in Urban Search and Rescue very easily might not have happened. The inspiring thing about these two public servants is how things did work out.

Despite the challenges of inter-organizational politics, state and federal programmatic concerns, and the difficulty of an evolving program, the duo's dedication to each other and the mission (with a little bit of luck and help along the way) provides a great tale.

I came to know Bob and Aris, or maybe better put, Aris and Bob, as a leader of the search component of California Task Force 5, which is a local, state, and DHS/FEMA National Urban Search and Rescue Response Program asset. It was my job to develop depth in the Canine Search component for all three. The effort was no easy task. In those days, bringing together a remarkably diverse professional skill set of groups and individuals was rife with disagreement.

Into this effort Aris and Bob, despite many obstacles, persevered. Long, arduous hours were spent to not only qualify but maintain certification. Of course, this was a collateral duty; they had a day job too that was as challenging as any.

Aris and Bob were always ready when the call came, including on 9/11, and they represented their organization, task force, and program well. Among many stories of valor and sacrifice, they served their country honorably, as you will read.

Sadly, as can be the case with such work, the effects of exposure to environmental and chemical substances on disaster scenes would later claim the life of many, canines, as well as first responders, far too early. Aris and service canines like him will always be remembered for bringing the last measure of sacrifice in all they do for the sheer love of their partner and in the joy of their rescue work.

This story of Aris and Bob will only strengthen that legacy; enjoy the read.

INTRODUCTION

September 11th, 2001, is a day that the world will never forget. America lost many lives that tragic day and it has forever changed us as a country. It's altered how we conduct our daily lives, added new security measures to public life, and forced us to sacrifice some of our freedoms — sacrifices intended to prevent another tragic event of such magnitude.

As we approach the 20th anniversary of those dreadful attacks, we know that these changes have made us a more difficult target for terrorists. We're now willing to wait in long lines for travel and consent to searches of our bodies and property.

We accept these inconveniences as the cost each of us pays to maintain that vigilance and safety. We're a stronger nation because of everyone's willingness to pull together against a common threat.

But even strong nations are tested. Today America feels more divided than I can ever remember. The unity we felt after 9/11 has receded with the passage of time. We cannot fight the evil in this world as a house divided. My hope is that we can put aside our differences and again unite, honoring the memory of those who sacrificed and died on 9/11. We need to set an example for the rest of the world to root out and conquer evil where it exists.

The events I experienced in the aftermath of 9/11 changed my life. I had just started a new phase of my career in law enforcement, as a narcotics investigator, when the towers fell. Immediately, I knew this extraordinary time called for me to step off my new path, if only temporarily, and apply the training I'd learned in the previous decade as a canine handler for the Orange County Sheriff's Department.

More importantly, I could only do it with my partner, himself recently on a new path: Aris, a 110-pound black Czech shepherd who had worked alongside me for seven years, fighting crime in our community and eventually becoming an elite search-and-rescue dog. Aris had been enjoying a hard-earned retirement in my family home. In the hours after the 9/11 attacks, Aris and I would team up for one last act.

It's taken me almost 20 years to write this book. Long hours of surveillance and serving search warrants didn't leave much time for writing, but after retiring in 2016, I felt it was time to tell the story of the true American hero whom I was fortunate enough to work alongside. Aris taught me lessons that I try to live by today, including the value of a hard work ethic and unconditional love for family and friends.

I was also moved to write this book by a recent visit to the 9/11 Memorial & Museum in New York City, my first return to Ground Zero since my deployment there after the attacks. I wanted readers to feel, as I did, a renewed sense of urgency to work together, to fend off acts of evil here at home and elsewhere in the world.

This book concentrates on my response to New York City on 9/11. That is what I personally experienced, yet in no way should it diminish the efforts and sacrifices of Americans at the Pentagon or aboard United Airlines Flight 93, the plane that tragically crashed into a field in Pennsylvania. Many Americans answered the call that day and went above and beyond the call of duty.

I also hope to highlight the contributions of people who trained Aris and me to such a level that we were able to assist in the New York rescue efforts. Through the eyes of a first responder, I want to give you a look into the unique life of my canine partner before, during, and after 9/11. And finally, I hope to show how Americans rallied in a time of unprecedented crisis, and how it's still in us to do it again.

Table of Contents

CHAPTER ONE

A MORNING I WILL NOT FORGET

On the morning of September 11th, 2001, my wife, Laura, and I were awakened by our 13-year-old son, Bryan. He'd been listening to the radio in his room as he was getting ready for school. Bryan walked into our bedroom, wiping sleep from his half-shut eyes, and said, "I think a plane just crashed into one of the Twin Towers in New York." I turned on the TV and watched in horror as the news replayed footage of American Airlines Flight 11 striking the North Tower of the World Trade Center. At 9:03 a.m., I watched in real time as United Airlines Flight 175 struck the South Tower. In disbelief, I realized this was no accident, but a deliberate act of terrorism.

I dressed and left for work. Listening to the radio while driving in, I heard about the collapse of both towers. Now I was anxious just to get to the station and learn more about the events that seemed to be unfolding by the minute.

When I arrived, I found everyone standing around televisions, trying to make sense of what was happening. Soon we'd learn that a third plane, American Airlines Flight 77, had crashed into the Pentagon, and later that a fourth plane, United Airlines Flight 93, went down in a field in Pennsylvania.

The news was crippling and hard to understand. No one knew how many people had been injured or killed. One thing soon became clear to me, though. Based on the staggering images of devastation, it was only a matter of time before my canine partner Aris and I would be summoned to New York to assist in the search and rescue efforts.

Let me back up here and give you some background on me and Aris, and the many hours and days of training that led to our deployment following that tragic day.

CHAPTER TWO

FINDING MY WAY

I joined the Orange County Sheriff's Department in January 1986. I was 25 years old and becoming a deputy wasn't part of the plan. Originally, I'd intended to graduate from college and apply to either law school or the Federal Bureau of Investigation (FBI).

After doing the math, I ruled out law school. Working as a waiter through college, I knew the pay probably wasn't enough to cover law school tuition. Besides, California seemed saturated with attorneys already.

The FBI sounded appealing, but I really didn't want to live anywhere other than Southern California. Then I realized there was a place where I could pursue the investigative work I longed to do without moving around the country. All I needed to do was get hired by the sheriff's department.

I'd been married all of four months when I was hired as a deputy, and I don't think my wife, Laura, was totally on-board with a profession that required me to wear a gun every day, including off duty, and to have a weapon in our home. But she wanted me to be happy in my work, and her support and willingness to see how this new journey would turn out is a testament to simply how amazing she is. Looking back now, I think it turned out remarkably well.

Academy graduation 1986

Deputy sheriffs are no different from police officers who work in cities, except that deputies have jurisdiction throughout their county, while city officers are restricted to their town's borders. Another difference is that deputies are first assigned to work in a jail before moving to patrol.

After graduating from the academy, my first assignment was at The Farm, a minimum-security jail in south Orange County. Officially the James A. Musick Branch Jail, named for the sheriff who served the county for nearly 30 years starting in the late 1940s, "The Farm" is an actual working farm, with crops and livestock raised within its 100-acre parcel tucked away in the northern corner of Irvine, California. Most people don't even know it exists.

Inmates at The Farm learn skills such as tractor-driving, planting and harvesting corn, and caring for the chickens, pigs, and cattle scattered around the property. There are worse places to do time.

Musick was a great place to start as a young deputy since I could interact with people in custody on a variety of charges. I could talk to them and begin to understand their behavior. Unlike a typical jail where inmates are locked behind cell doors, The Farm allowed me to walk and work among the inmates.

I quickly had to develop a command presence, an ability to stand in front of the prisoners, issue commands, and keep order, without showing signs of nerves or intimidation. I would walk into one of the temporary tents housing 200 inmates, with maybe just two deputies to keep order, and call on all my reserves of communication skills, especially since I weighed all of about 130 pounds after graduating from the academy.

Inmates could sense if you were weak or unsure of yourself and would play games with you to make your job that much harder. The inmates could also turn on you quickly if you overstepped your bounds, but I always tried to treat them fairly, and most of them respected that.

Working in the jail soon revealed some of the dark edges of life and death. I was patrolling the facility perimeter one day when a "man down" call came over the radio. I rushed to the scene to find an inmate lying on the restroom floor, bleeding from one of his wrists. My partner and I checked for a pulse but couldn't detect one. I rolled the man over and noticed that he'd slit his wrist with a blade pulled from a disposable razor. This was my first, and unfortunately not last, encounter with someone taking his own life.

Our homicide unit soon responded and questioned everyone at the scene. I went home and had several bad dreams for the next few nights. Seeing death occur in this manner tends to remain in your thoughts for quite some time.

I spent three-and-a-half years working in the jail, and the experience made me a better deputy. The knowledge I gained from my rapport with the inmates helped once I started on patrol. On the streets, I'd often run into individuals I knew from the jail. Sometimes they'd even remember me. In jail, I remember watching inmates break some rule or steal an apple from the chow hall right in front of me, then lie when confronted about it. I couldn't believe the stories they'd make up on the spot. If I hadn't witnessed the offense myself, I just might have bought their story.

Dealing with this kind of criminal cunning in the jail helped me when talking to people on the streets. I learned to not take what they said at face value, but probe deeper and ask questions to get to the truth.

In the jail, I also learned the language of tattoos and how to distinguish between jail, prison, or gang ink. While talking to people with these tattoos out on the streets, I could place them in a gang, or maybe a certain neighborhood, or discern whether the tattoo was drug-related.

When I'd ask about their tattoos, they knew they couldn't feed me a story about where they came from, and they tended to talk more freely than they might to someone who didn't understand the tattoo meanings.

Most of the inmates respected that I treated them fairly, so when they saw me on the street, they didn't hold a grudge. I'd spend time talking to them; sometimes they'd even tell me information that helped solve a particular crime I was investigating.

CHAPTER THREE

K-9 CHANGES MY CAREER PATH

The sheriff's department patrols the unincorporated areas of a county, and after my jail assignment I was sent to patrol Laguna Niguel, a quiet, affluent city in south Orange County. The area is mostly comprised of residential homes and shopping centers, and crime is low. What crime did exist typically included property crimes such as burglary and theft.

On some midnight shifts (the rookie always gets stuck on these shifts), I'd drive 100 miles around the same areas looking for crime in a community that only measures about 15 square miles. Sometimes things were so slow that I'd be assigned crossing guard duty at a local elementary school.

Meanwhile, I got to know several of my area partners who were canine handlers. It seemed that they always got the good calls — crimes in progress, robberies, suspicious subjects possibly burglarizing homes — while I was stuck writing reports.

I started to rethink my position and became very interested in the dogs and their handlers. I'd watch them roll in each night driving their own patrol cars, clearly marked with the canine stickers on the sides and "K-9" written on the roof (used to help our helicopter units know which car had a dog). The cars were cool, but I was also impressed by the work ethic. It was rare that a handler ever called in sick for a shift.

The dogs were also always eager to get out and search, or perform any task asked of them.

The canine handlers also appeared to be in great physical shape. They were all older than me and I wondered how they were in such good shape. I became better friends with several of the handlers the longer we worked together and eventually started hanging out with them off-duty. One day they invited me to go mountain biking and I quickly realized that the biking, combined with the canine training, was a key reason for their fitness. As someone who was, and remains, physically active, this kind of work looked appealing.

Even more appealing was that canine handlers could take their patrol cars home at the end of a shift. Gas prices in Southern California were pretty high then, and for a young deputy with a family, a "company car" could mean a helpful financial lift.

I do remember worrying that if I had a take-home car, my neighbors would end up seeing me drive a black-and-white into my garage every night. It can be a good thing or a bad thing when everyone in the neighborhood knows you're a police officer. Regardless, I was still very interested and started asking plenty of questions about how to join my friends as a canine handler for the department.

The canine team would train every Wednesday at different locations throughout Orange County, and I started to attend some of the sessions during my time off. The team usually met at a regional park for the first half of training, then moved to some abandoned or empty buildings for the second half.

Being the new guy, I was volunteered as "the suspect" on several of the canine searches, which meant wearing a bite suit and either running or hiding from the dogs. This was a little unnerving at first. The handler would dress me up in a padded suit, then hide me somewhere often dark and very secluded. There I'd just sit and wait. And wait.

Sometimes I'd hear the handler make an announcement ordering me to surrender:

"Attention in the building. This is the Orange County Sheriff's Department. Come out now or we will send a dog in to find you."

The handler would repeat this three times before saying: "This is your final warning. Surrender now or I will send in the dog and he may bite you."

Hiding inside a building, I could hear the dog's feet tapping on the concrete floor as it came closer to my location. I could also hear the dog using its nose to locate my scent. Once it had zeroed in on my hiding spot, the dog would bark and continue barking. It's trained to do this; barking, rather than immediately biting a subject, both protects the dog and helps the handler pinpoint the location of the subject.

If the dog bit a subject right away, the handler might not know where to find the dog, or if the dog had even located anyone. The dogs were trained to bite only if the subject tried to run, or if the subject physically attacked them.

This training also teaches the dogs that protecting their handler is an important part of their job. The dogs will try to apprehend anyone that appears to threaten (shove or aggressively charge, for example) the handler.

In training, the dogs would continue to bark until the handlers arrived, and once they did, I would either surrender or try to outrun the dogs. This gave them an opportunity to chase me down and apprehend me, which they loved. I was amazed how each dog worked the scent trail until they found me. They made it seem easy and appeared to enjoy it.

I learned quite a bit by hiding, but also by watching the handlers as they worked their dogs. These dogs are motivated to search by their "prey drive," which means they're actually hunting. This is a survival instinct that is second only to their reproductive drive. Later, this prey drive would come into play during my training and searching on 9/11.

I assisted with canine training for a couple of years, and in 1992, a new opening for a handler came up. This was a very coveted position, and the selection process included an oral interview and a written internal position request. A sergeant from the K-9 unit also came out to my home to visually inspect the yard, ensuring it had enough space for a kennel and that the dog could be secured.

During the interview, I was asked if my neighbors would tolerate living next door to a police canine. Believe it or not, some people don't want to be near a dog known to bite! I was also asked situational questions related to releasing the dog. Dogs are considered a use of force and are therefore subject to the laws and policies regulating that use. You shouldn't release a dog on a shoplifter, for example (a misdemeanor crime), or even a subject who has just vandalized a building with graffiti. Every situation was different, but typically the dogs were reserved for apprehending felons or someone acting violent.

The dogs were also used as a search tool to save man-hours for the department. A dog could clear a building (meaning no live human scent was found inside) in just five minutes, where it would take five deputies about 30 minutes to do the same. Considering we'd respond to several alarm calls on any given shift, this was time well-saved. On many alarm calls, we'd respond to find an open door and a building that needed to be cleared. Dogs were the most efficient and safest way to clear these buildings.

I passed the interviews and got the job as the new canine handler. I was super excited to see exactly what kind of dog I would get. The current K-9 unit had a variety of dogs, including German shepherds, a Dutch shepherd, and a Belgian Malinois. As a brand-new canine handler, I was able to go to the kennels and have a minor say in which dog became my future partner.

I drove to Adlerhorst Kennels, about an hour away in Riverside County, with Steve Sligh, the handler I would be replacing. Most of the police agencies got their dogs from Adlerhorst, and owner Dave Reaver was an expert at the selection and training of police canines.

Mr. Reaver had great insights into canine behaviors and what was needed to train new handlers. It seemed like the dogs already knew what to do, and so handlers just needed to learn how to understand what the dogs were doing. We looked at several dogs that day, and one of them, "Rocky," a three-year-old Belgian Malinois, stood out from the rest. He just seemed to have the most energy. We chose Rocky and loaded him into my very own canine unit. I brought him home and introduced him to my family, and I remember the kids being so excited about having a new dog, even if they were a little nervous about playing with a dog that bites bad guys for a living.

Rocky came from Holland, so all of my commands to him were in Dutch. I learned about 15 different words that ranged from obedience to protection commands. This was not, as you might think, to prevent a suspect from commanding him in English. Dutch was simply the language Rocky learned growing up, the same as you or me learning the language where we're raised.

Even in the unlikely event we happened on a Dutch-speaking suspect, Rocky wouldn't listen to or obey the person. A dog only has one alpha — a person or another dog in charge — that he or she needs to listen to. I was Rocky's alpha and that was all he needed.

CHAPTER FOUR

K-9 BASIC TRAINING

Rocky and I went through a basic four-week canine training and developed a strong bond. During this time, a handler spends more time with the dog than with his or her own family, and it's amazing to watch this bond develop. I was told to take Rocky home, feed him and play with him, but that was all I should do. The trainers told me not to give him too many commands for at least one week. This was to focus Rocky on associating me with his feeding and play time, and eventually build up trust between the two of us. He could trust that I would show up every day with a bowl of food, take him for walks, and play with him. This was my first experience creating that kind of bond with a dog I'd just met, and it was different from the one I had with my childhood pet.

When I was very young, my sisters and I would play with our Weimaraner puppy Duke every day. Duke loved playing with everyone. But a police dog is a working dog and bonds with just one person. This bond is a unique and special relationship that only the handler gets to experience with his or her partner.

During the training, I met officers from other agencies also learning to become handlers. Most of us were first-timers; I can remember only one officer who was working with his second dog.

The training sessions included classroom study covering use of force, liability, and search patterns and techniques, but mostly it was hands-on work with the dogs. We started each day with obedience training, as our instructor would have us walk up and down the field making left turns, right turns, about turns (180 degrees), and stops. Establishing obedience was key to our training because if your dog did not respect or listen to you, then you'd never be able to control the dog in the field. And because our dogs would work as "apprehension dogs," there was a great deal of liability to each department, and handler, if something went wrong.

Unlike a narcotics or bomb detection dog, which is trained to search for the odor of certain chemicals or narcotics, an apprehension dog searches specifically for live humans. And the only way a dog apprehends a person is by clamping down and holding on. No department wants to be sued and most try to minimize that risk through training. Orange County is a pretty conservative area and most agencies in the county didn't want to take any chance of a dog biting an innocent civilian. That's why we trained our dogs to guard and bark. Rocky, for example, was trained to locate a subject, then bark when he succeeded. He was not allowed to simply run in, find suspects, then bite them.

We accomplished this with handlers standing in blinds (wooden structures with one open side) and sending Rocky to find them. When he came around the corner and found his subject, he had to bark. If he tried to get too close or bite the subject, the handler would use two bamboo sticks to stop him. The sticks could be crossed in front of the handler, or if the dog was too aggressive, the handler would quickly swat at the dog. This way, the dog would learn to keep a short distance from the subject and not bite right away.

Rocky quickly learned that it was better to bark and wait for my arrival than to rush in. Once Rocky had barked for a certain length of time, the subject would either run or try to attack the dog. Either of those scenarios gave Rocky the green light to bite the subject.

Rocky always seemed fixated on the training equipment rather than the trainer acting as a suspect, though. This was a bit of a red flag, and it became an issue not only in training but later on in the field as well. But I still had high hopes for him. He was full of energy and drive.

After graduating from basic training, Rocky and I were assigned to patrol the unincorporated area of Aliso Viejo. We responded to calls like any other patrol unit (except traffic accidents, which were handled by the California Highway Patrol) and stayed very busy, as our area tended to be understaffed. Some of the cities around Aliso Viejo began to incorporate, and the sheriff's department needed to ensure an adequate number of patrol cars were covering the newly incorporated cities. Sometimes deputies were pulled from the unincorporated areas to fill the gaps.

Remember I told you about Rocky's fixation with the training equipment? The bite sleeve, one of several pieces of equipment we used, is a sleeve that our "actors" wore to protect against puncture wounds from the dog's teeth. Made of thick burlap, the sleeve had a metal handle inside the hand grip that the actor could grasp, and also a hard plastic portion just above the elbow to protect the upper arm.

Rocky really seemed to love the bite sleeve more than he did the actual suspect. I would send Rocky to bite one of our actors, who would then drop the sleeve once I'd arrived and taken hold of the dog. Rocky lost all interest in the actor and just wanted to bite the sleeve!

This did not translate well to his searches in the field. More than once Rocky would find a suspect in hiding, only to move on when he noticed the suspect was not wearing any equipment. This became a serious problem, and after three years of us working together, Rocky was granted an early retirement. I gave him to a colleague who owned six acres of fenced property where Rocky could chase rabbits every day. After his short career in police work, Rocky was extremely happy in his new home.

CHAPTER FIVE

A PERFECT PARTNER

Randy McLennan, one of the department's previous canine handlers who'd later been promoted to sergeant and had since left the canine unit, called me one day. Randy was working in a city that contracted with the sheriff's department and told me that he'd spoken with his lieutenant, Kim Markuson, about bringing a canine to the city of Mission Viejo. Knowing Randy, this meant that he'd taken the time and effort to pitch the idea to the city leaders. He was the kind of guy who wanted the canine program to be successful, but would never be one to take credit when it was.

At that time, all of the department's canines patrolled the county's unincorporated areas. Cities in south Orange County had just started contracting with the sheriff's department for police services, but none of these contracts had yet provided for a canine unit dedicated to the individual city. This was super exciting to me because it meant that I would actually be assigned to patrol Mission Viejo.

Randy and Lt. Markuson also wanted to create a roving canine position within the city, meaning that I'd be free from normal calls (traffic collisions and report calls, such as theft, vandalism, assault, or various other crimes — important calls, but not ones that required a canine) and be able to respond to more serious calls such as crimes in progress. This was very innovative thinking on Randy and Lt. Markuson's part, and Mission Viejo definitely had the resources to fund this type of position. Now all I needed was a new dog.

Fortunately, the community also saw the benefits of a local canine unit. The local Elks Lodge held a weekly bingo night that raised enough money — more than $15,000 — to cover the costs of a dog and training. I asked Mr. Reaver at Adlerhorst Kennels if he could look for a Czech shepherd on his next trip to Europe. Reaver would often go there to find dogs for law enforcement agencies, rather than look in the United States. European breeders tend to be better at tracking a dog's family history, meaning you know exactly what type of dog you're getting. They also have referees that maintain the pure lines of each breed. If you want to breed your dog, you first need to get it approved by the referee. This protects a dog's pedigree and leaves a paper trail so that each new owner can verify the dog's history.

From my initial training with Rocky, I remembered an officer from another city who had a Czech shepherd. It was an amazing dog. Dogs from the Czech Republic were sometimes used as sentry dogs, which the Czech army would use to patrol and guard the country's border. Compared to the traditional German shepherd, which had been bred for show (its signature sloping back causes serious hip problems for many shepherds as they age), the Czech shepherd was bred for protection. In 1956, Jiri Novotny established a program in Czechoslovakia that focused on breeding quality canines with the most desirable traits for protection, including, but not limited to, strengthening the dogs' bones, ensuring proper temperament, developing strong nerves, and an ability to work in tracking, obedience, and protection.

Mr. Reaver called after one of his trips and suggested I visit the kennels to look at one of the dogs he'd brought back. Randy and I drove out to the kennels, and as we walked to the back portion of Mr. Reaver's property, I noticed several other law enforcement agencies already there, looking at different dogs. Anytime Mr. Reaver returned from Europe, everyone hurried to his kennels to get first dibs on the best dogs.

Mr. Reaver brought out a huge black shepherd that looked like a bear and handed me the leash. He told me to walk the dog around, and as soon as I did, the dog tried to bite me. I immediately fell in love with it. I was not wearing any training equipment, and unlike Rocky, this dog did not need any equipment in order to take an interest in me.

I know it sounds a little crazy, but it was a welcome change from Rocky. Prior to purchase, one of the tests we'd run through with a dog was to show it a bite sleeve, see how it reacted, and test its bite on the sleeve. If a dog is tentative on the bite, it can mean it has bad teeth or is not sure of itself. This dog had a very strong bite and beautiful teeth.

Another test involved a subject running quite a distance away; then we'd send the dog in a full-speed chase to bite the runner. This allowed us to see how fast the dog could run and if there were any problems with its gait or biting ability. This dog ran down the runner with ease and seemed very happy while doing it.

Some of you may know that the German shepherd breed is known to be very smart and sometimes almost too perfect. Most will only apprehend a suspect by the arm, as they are trained to do in Germany. This dog, on the other hand, seemed like it would bite you anywhere.

I walked the dog back to Mr. Reaver and asked him its name. He told me his name was Aris, and that he was three years old. I looked at Aris's paperwork (his registration), which is like a birth certificate, which showed that he was born April 15, 1992, in Hungary. There he was named Ordog, which means "devil" in Hungarian. I was glad that someone had changed his name to Aris.

I was told that all of Aris's commands were in Czech, so I needed to learn about 15 new words. We purchased Aris that day, and little did I know that he would be such an amazing partner and become a much loved member of my family forever.

I brought Aris home and introduced him to Laura and the kids: seven-year-old Bryan, four-year-old Kelsey, and two-year-old Garrett. Everyone loved Aris because he was so big, yet so friendly. He was truly a beautiful specimen of the shepherd family.

Before I could take Aris out on the street, however, we had to complete the basic training course. Having already gone through the training once helped me concentrate more fully on Aris this time, since I already knew the program. Training with Aris was amazing. He was not always the most obedient dog, but he made up for it in his drive to search and apprehend.

Aris was already "Schutzhund 1-certified." In Germany, people raise dogs and train them in the art of obedience, tracking, and protection, with the goal of certifying a dog as "Schutzhund 3" and creating a champion. Aris's great-grandparents were both Schutzhund 3-certified. (The United Schutzhund Clubs of America defines schutzhund standards as those that measure a dog's mental stability, endurance, courage, willingness to work, and trainability, among other traits. A more detailed explanation is available in Appendix A at the back of the book.)

Once a dog was certified, the owner would sell it to people like Mr. Reaver, who would then sell the dog to one of the law enforcement agencies in the United States. Since the certified dogs were already trained in tracking (following human scent and finding its source), protection (defending their handler), and obedience, they fit very nicely into the needs of law enforcement.

Aris was just as I thought he would be in training: fearless. Unlike other shepherds that would only apprehend suspects by an arm if available, Aris would grab an arm or leg, the chest, or whatever was available to him. I was pretty excited about this part of his character and Aris quickly developed a reputation in training. Remember, Rocky was only interested in the equipment. Aris couldn't have cared less about the equipment. He always tried to get under or through the equipment and get to the suspect. Other handlers that would hide from Aris during training needed to completely cover up in the bite suit. If they left a body part or appendage exposed, Aris would find it! He was not afraid to grab you anywhere.

His deep bark alone was enough to make most people give up and not want to suffer a bite. Aris also had a very keen sense of smell, which helped him find anyone or anything in hiding. In addition, he had a different way of starting his searches than most other dogs. He would usually take a few steps into the search area, then come back to me and bark, inviting me to come with him. He did this on almost all building searches or large area searches where he would have to leave my sight. This behavior would show up often in our training and testing during our time as partners.

It was unique behavior, and I think it was just his way of communicating with me. He definitely was not afraid to venture out alone. He was always confident and courageous in all that he did. I would usually just give him a command to search again and he would go out on his own.

CHAPTER SIX

BACK ON THE STREETS

After training, I was excited to be back on the street in a new position, with my new partner, Aris. A few months later we became Mission Viejo's roving canine unit, and we were generally free to respond to priority calls or crimes in progress, as long as there were other patrol cars available to take standard report calls. This freed me and Aris to back up deputies who needed assistance or respond to searches for suspects who had run or hidden from deputies.

It didn't take long for Aris to apprehend his first suspect. Deputies had stopped a male subject driving a small truck. The driver was refusing commands and threatening the deputies with a long metal rod. I arrived on the scene and positioned Aris where the subject could see him as well as hear my announcements. I made several announcements asking for the subject to comply with our orders, but he continued to refuse the orders and raised the metal bar in his hand.

I gave Aris the command to search and sent him toward the vehicle. When he was about four feet from the vehicle, I gave Aris the command to bite the suspect. Still wielding the metal rod, the suspect jumped back into the truck, but not fast enough; Aris managed to grab the suspect by his leg and "persuade" him out of the vehicle, where he was swiftly taken into custody.

I was impressed by Aris's ability to focus on the suspect in the vehicle, while blocking out the distraction of 10 deputies standing around yelling at the suspect. By using Aris to apprehend the suspect, we avoided any injuries to the deputies, and any further injury to a suspect who was resisting arrest. This was the beginning of a beautiful relationship, and Aris impressed me every time he got out of the car.

Lt. Markuson was also impressed with Aris and recognized his potential to be cross-trained as a narcotics detection dog. This was also very innovative thinking because the sheriff's department did not, at that time, have any dogs cross-trained in both apprehension and narcotics. Training Aris this way would mean a narcotics dog would be available to assist deputies almost every day. At that time, most dogs assigned to a narcotics detail were often tied up on a case and unavailable for a quick response.

Lt. Markuson with Aris and me

Deputies can only detain someone for a limited time without probable cause, so a cross-trained canine already in the field could respond to a request for a narcotics search within minutes. Lt. Markuson would ultimately sell the idea to both the sheriff's department and Mission Viejo city leaders. Again, the City of Mission Viejo had the resources to make this happen, so once we'd convinced the department, Aris and I enrolled in the narcotics training course. I think the department worried that the dogs wouldn't be able to distinguish between searching for drugs and searching for a suspect. Again, liability was a chief concern.

Searching for drugs is a game, and the dogs search out of their play drive, unlike the prey drive used to search for suspects. Narcotics training began with handlers making plastic toys for the dogs to play with. These toys were made from a piece of pipe with caps screwed onto both ends. I would remove the caps and place a specific drug — marijuana, cocaine, heroin, methamphetamine — in the pipe. The pipes were drilled with small holes to allow odor to escape.

I would play catch and tug-of-war with Aris using one of the pipes (the drugs were secured inside the pipe with no chance of leaking out and possibly affecting Aris). After playing for a while, I would stick the pipe under my boot and make Aris scratch and dig for it, and after he scratched for a minute, I would let him play with it. The idea was that while Aris was chewing on the toy, his keen sense of smell would pick up on the narcotic odor being released. Aris soon associated the pipe and each of the narcotic odors with play and fun. I'd hide the pipe in increasingly difficult locations, then walk him around the area and give him a different command than I used when searching for suspects.

I would tell him "find it," and when he located the plastic pipe, he would scratch. As soon as he did, I'd throw a chew toy (a small piece of wrapped burlap) at the location where he was scratching. Soon Aris would learn to associate that scratching where the drugs were hidden would make his chew toy magically appear. Pretty simple concept, but we increased the difficulty by hiding the drugs in high places and inside concealed compartments.

Just like with apprehension training, Aris was very aggressive during narcotics detection training and proved he could find drugs as well as, if not better than, most of the dogs trained specifically for the task. This was a huge step in preparing our dogs to be cross-trained for duties other than apprehension, and ultimately opened the door for Aris and me to train for urban search and rescue.

After graduating from narcotics school, Aris and I returned to the streets of Mission Viejo. We had many great experiences while on patrol, but one of my favorite memories actually happened just outside our city borders. In the quiet neighboring city of Rancho Santa Margarita, a man walked up behind another and shot him in the head. The victim was rushed to the hospital, while the suspect was last seen running toward the community lake. The lead deputy asked me to have Aris search the area around the lake for the gun that the shooter may have used in the attack, then ditched.

In addition to his ability to find people and drugs, Aris could find objects marked with human scent, even just a very small amount (he was great for finding my keys if I lost them in the yard). We trained our dogs to find articles like handguns and other weapons, which required a different search command so the dogs would know to search for an object, not a person or drugs. I used the Dutch word to search, which is zoeken. I am sure I did not pronounce it correctly, but it sounded something like "sucha."

This command was strictly for article searches and, because we trained every week on these searches, Aris knew exactly what to do. The search area was huge, covering a 1.1-mile loop of grass and ivy surrounding the lake. There was a slight breeze that night, so I walked Aris along the edge of the lake near the ivy plants. About 50 yards into our walk, Aris began turning his head toward the ivy and pulling me toward a certain area. The location was near a major roadway and in the middle of some heavy ivy growth.

I watched Aris bury his nose into the ivy and heard him crunch down on something solid. I immediately told him to release the object and walked over to find a shiny metal revolver on the ground. I couldn't believe it — Aris had just found a needle in a haystack! It never ceased to amaze me what he and the other dogs could do.

I notified the deputy in charge, who then had our identification and forensic experts collect and photograph the revolver. At this point, I didn't know if this was the gun used in the shooting, but I knew that, at the very least, Aris had taken a gun off the street, possibly preventing it from being used against someone else.

Aris and I then searched the walkway entrance of an apartment believed to be connected to the shooter. Deputies had searched the area already but wanted to double-check it with the dog. Aris had already proven himself by finding the first gun, and deputies thought he might find something they had missed.

They were right. About two steps into our search, Aris turned into the deep ivy and again I saw his head disappear, then I heard the crunch as his mouth bit down on something solid. I told him to release, he obeyed, and I walked over to find a black semi-automatic handgun. I searched around nearby and also found a pack of cigarettes and a disposable camera.

I had our identification technicians respond, photograph, and collect the items as evidence. What an incredible night for Aris, locating two guns when nobody else could find them — guns that, as it turned out, belonged to the two suspects! One of the guns had been used to shoot the victim, and the disposable camera had pictures of both suspects holding their respective guns. You couldn't have asked for better evidence.

This was just one example of the amazing feats Aris could perform when called into action. His reputation grew, and more deputies began calling on him to search for suspects or articles of evidence.

One time while I happened to be on duty, the gang unit requested a narcotics detection dog. I responded to the call, and when I arrived

I saw several deputies searching a small pickup truck. The lead gang investigator explained that he had solid information indicating that drugs were hidden somewhere in the truck, yet deputies had torn it apart and come up empty.

Now, when you read about narcotic detection dogs that sniff out hundreds of kilograms of cocaine, you think, "That dog is amazing." And while Aris had his share of large finds, that quantity of cocaine will saturate an area with its odor. It's actually a fairly easy find for the dog. The more difficult and impressive finds are the smaller amounts that require the dog's most finely honed senses and instinct.

I cleared everyone away from the truck and began walking Aris around the vehicle. He didn't alert or show any interest on the first walk around the truck. I walked him around a second time. This time as we came around to the engine compartment (the hood was open and it had already been searched), Aris lifted his nose toward the engine. I stopped, and Aris stood on his back legs and took a couple good sniffs of the engine compartment.

On his own, all 110 pounds of him leapt up into the engine compartment (I told you he was passionate and had a strong drive), and after he stumbled around for a minute, he stuck his head down toward the firewall. After he bit down on and pulled off a metal cylinder attached to the firewall, several plastic baggies of methamphetamine fell from the container. The cylinder perfectly matched other items that belonged in the engine bay, right down to the dirt covering it, and it attached to the firewall with a magnet. It wasn't just a regular metal container attached to the truck — we'd seen many of those before — but was instead a legitimate mechanical part that belonged on the truck.

The gang guys were extremely happy to recover about 15 grams of methamphetamine, which may not sound like much, but holds up as one of Aris's best finds. The cross-training had paid off and everyone was pleased with his performance.

Aris had a phenomenal career, which also included a bit of public relations. He and I did hundreds of "officer friendlies" where we'd go to schools ranging from kindergarten to high school. I would demonstrate how Aris could find people, articles, and drugs. For the older kids we would stage a hidden suspect. Aris would find the suspect, who would then run, and Aris would give chase at full speed. This was always a crowd pleaser.

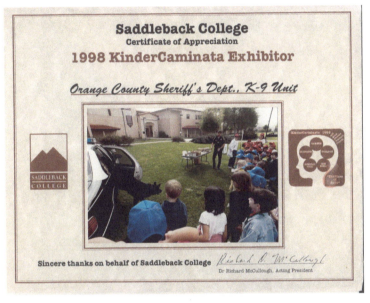

Aris would always tolerate kids pulling and tugging on him, and petting him, but when it came time to work, he was ready. Word about Aris had spread to numerous schools and even a local community college. Saddleback Valley College (now known simply as Saddleback College) had a student-created television series called "Around the Town." The film crew came to one of our canine training sessions and saw firsthand how well we controlled the dogs and how incredible their search skills were. The crew even came to my house and interviewed my daughter, Kelsey, and youngest son, Garrett. The kids were very enthusiastic while talking about Aris and how much they loved him.

As I mentioned before, Aris's bark was intimidating, not only in training but to all the suspects he encountered. Many would give up right away rather than discover what was on the other side of that bark. Deputies could point guns at a suspect all day and night, yet the suspect might still refuse to comply with their orders. Once Aris and I arrived on scene and he got out of the car and started to bark, suspects often gave up immediately. The few times they didn't (usually while under the influence of drugs) or when they became aggressive or threatening toward deputies, I would make an announcement and then send Aris to apprehend the suspect.

In one memorable instance, a suspect had stolen a vehicle, then approached me in a threatening manner, refusing all commands to stop. I released Aris and sent him on a bite command. The suspect was wearing a heavy jacket and Aris bit him in the arm. The suspect was high on something strong enough that allowed him to ignore the pain and he actually started punching Aris in the head, asking the dog, "Is that all you got?!"

No, Aris had plenty more. Not one to shy away from a fight, Aris released the suspect's arm, then bit him on the unprotected inner thigh. The suspect immediately screamed and fell to the ground, where he was handcuffed and taken into custody. Aris was physically fine, other than a little angry at the suspect, even after the incident was over. As I said, biting a suspect was rare, simply because his size and bark were already so intimidating.

Aris's ability to turn this aggression on and off was a major factor when I decided to train him for search and rescue. As you'll see later, there were civilians standing on the rubble piles that Aris was assigned to search, so he needed to know that he was expected to look for someone buried beneath the debris, not someone standing on top of the pile.

CHAPTER SEVEN

ONE VERY TALENTED DOG

One day I was reading *Police*, a magazine that covered police work, when an article caught my attention, detailing how one department certified its canine unit for FEMA Urban Search and Rescue. The Federal Emergency Management Agency has urban search and rescue teams throughout the United States. I thought of the threats we face here in Southern California from earthquakes and land movement, and how it would be great for our department to have dogs trained to search the kind of environments we'd face in the event of building collapses and mudslides, and hopefully save lives. Here it's not a matter of if we have a significant earthquake, but rather "when" and "how big."

So I read up on how I could certify our dogs for search and rescue with FEMA and quickly learned that, as with any federal program, there was a lot of red tape and jumping through hoops to get certified as a canine search specialist.

But as I read the certification requirements for a canine search specialist, I realized that our dogs met nearly all the criteria. They'd just need some fine-tuning in certain areas, including the small detail of training them not to bite the evaluators or civilians who might also be in the search area. For this, we'd need to develop a new search command so the dogs would understand that this was a different kind of assignment than a standard suspect search.

I used a very simple phrase — "find 'em" — every time I searched, and I knew Aris could handle this new challenge since he'd done so well with the narcotics training. I was excited to add another skill to Aris's already impressive resumé.

Before you're eligible for the search portion of the certification test, you're required to complete some element testing. The elements test a dog's physical ability and obedience, and include tasks such as climbing a ladder and walking on uneven surfaces. Dogs also have to lie next to another dog for five minutes, out of sight of the handler, and aren't allowed to get up, leave the area, or get aggressive with other dogs.

These tests ensure that a dog can search independently, away from its handler, while avoiding injury. There's nothing worse when responding to a critical incident and searching for victims than for you or your dog to become victims yourselves and require extraction or medical aid. I'm not sure of the passing rate for the elements exam, but it is a rigorous portion of the national certification in urban search and rescue.   (Interested readers can find the required elements and tests in the document *National Urban Search and Rescue Response System: A Component of the National Response Framework Emergency Support Function 9, Canine Search Team Certification Evaluation Handbook Live Find*, available at www.disasterdog.org. This is the ultimate guidebook for the handler seeking to become FEMA-certified as a canine search specialist.)

After speaking with the other handlers on our department's canine unit, we judged that three of our dogs had the personality and talent for the tests. Using an apprehension dog to search around others is already risky, and we felt the other dogs just wouldn't have been friendly enough with FEMA evaluators on the rubble pile. So we picked Blek, belonging to my colleague Mike Gaard; Blitz, belonging to another colleague, Wayne Byerly; and Aris to start training for the tests.

This was all new to us, so we had to improvise and make some of our own training aids. We built homemade seesaws and ladders to practice on, and tunnels that required the dogs to crawl through on their bellies.

We signed up for our first element test, which included several uneven obstacles designed to make the dogs uncomfortable in their footing. There were also balance beams and a ladder that the dogs had to climb. Another element tested the dog's ability to take direction from its handler while being physically separated from the handler. You had to be able to send your dog to go in a certain direction and to a specific location, without stopping, and do it in a pattern determined by the person administering the test. These tests were designed to ensure that a dog could search through rubble safely and efficiently. Blek, Blitz, and Aris all passed.

With the element test under our belts, we concentrated on the rubble pile search. We practiced by burying volunteers beneath the rubble for the dogs to find. My oldest son, Bryan, was one of those volunteers, and on weekends I'd take him with us to a local rubble pile where I'd create a cave-like hiding place for him out of broken chunks of concrete marked for recycling. Then I'd carefully and completely (and safely, of course) cover him up, and finally give Aris his command — "find 'em" — and send him out on the pile. Aris would make quick work of the pile, negotiating large, uneven boulders of concrete, and upon locating Bryan's scent, he would start barking.

I would approach Aris and take hold of him while one of us uncovered the rubble pile enough that Bryan could extend the bite sleeve out of the opening. After I released Aris, he would bite the sleeve and play tug-of-war with Bryan. This may sound strange, but it had a purpose. Remember that the dogs are searching, hunting, for prey and if we don't reward them, they'll lose interest.

To train the dogs to remain at the site where they've alerted us to a find, we'd practice "sequential barking" exercises. I'd send Aris to search and once he found the victim and barked, I would immediately reward him with a bite. I would send him again, but this time make him bark 10 times before a reward, then again after 20 barks, and still again after barking five times, for example. Mixing up the reward requirement kept the dogs guessing, with the intention of training them to stay at their find and continue barking.

Bryan was a trooper and gave the rest of us a break from always playing the victim in our training scenarios. Coincidentally, it was Bryan, who also walked into our bedroom on 9/11 and asked me and Laura if we knew about the plane that had just crashed into one of the Twin Towers.

The sheriff's department was not really involved with our search and rescue training at this point, so we trained during our off-duty time. We were the first canine handlers within the department to consider training for these tests, so the department didn't quite know how to assist us. After all of our training, I felt Aris had mastered all obstacles and we were ready to take the test.

Occasionally, one of these FEMA-hosted certification events would be local to us. Some of the FEMA evaluators were concerned about apprehension dogs taking their test, and I couldn't really blame them. After all, our dogs were trained to bite. One person who helped calm that fear was Rob Patterson, a captain with the Orange County Fire Authority.

Rob was well aware of the sheriff's canine unit and we hit it off right away. He was able to smooth things over with FEMA personnel and guide us in the right direction. Rob was a huge asset and helped us integrate into the search and rescue program. I don't think we could've made it through the whole testing process without Rob paving the way.

For its basic Type 2 certification, FEMA requires a canine and its handler to find two victims buried beneath a rubble pile within 15 minutes. The handler must stay at the bottom of the pile until the dog alerts to its first find. Once the dog finds a victim, it must stay in the location and continue barking until the handler can arrive and direct the dog on the pile as needed.

Blek and Blitz both passed their tests. When Aris and I were up, I forgot to ask a key question prior to the search: "Is the power turned off?"

As you can imagine, this could be an important question in certain situations. I failed and wasn't allowed to search. The whole search and rescue program was new to me and there was a lot to remember, but I was disappointed to not pass and also a little embarrassed for not asking the proper questions. To their credit, Mike and Wayne didn't criticize me and immediately started to think about a future test date for me.

I also felt a little better when a FEMA representative later explained that my failure had actually helped improve their program. FEMA responded by developing a laminated card for handlers to carry with a checklist of questions to ask before a search, questions that would be consistent throughout the search and rescue program.

I had to wait a few months before my next opportunity to take the Type 2 test, but when it came, I jumped on it. Mike and I drove out to the test location in Bakersfield, California. I was nervous because my earlier failure was still fresh in mind, but now I had my handy laminated question card and knew I'd be fine, and that Aris would finally have a chance to search.

Mike and his wife, Christan, sat above the rubble pile with a video camera to record the entire search (I didn't know they'd be filming, only that they'd be watching from somewhere near the rubble). The canine handler isn't allowed to see the rubble pile, which measured approximately 40 yards long and 30 yards wide, prior to the test.

When it was my turn, I drove down a dirt road and was told to park off to the side of the pile. I was directed to an area sectioned off with yellow caution tape and told this was my starting area. I met with a FEMA evaluator for my briefing and as I stood at the base of the pile, I could see other FEMA evaluators at the top waiting to observe me and Aris. I began the briefing and went through the questions on my newly laminated card. Then I made an announcement in Aris's ear for him to search, and off he went.

Aris usually liked me to search alongside him, but that wasn't allowed for this kind of test. So Aris went out, then quickly returned and barked for me to join him. I sent him back out on his own with another search command, followed by an additional command to move farther out on the pile (directional training coming in handy here).

About a minute after sending him out, I heard his bark indicating that he had found live human scent buried under the rubble. I walked up the stacks of concrete boulders and found Aris in the middle of the pile, barking and trying to dig into the rubble (true to his nature as an apprehension dog). I praised him, saying "*hodny pes*" ("good dog" in Czech), then told the evaluator to direct search and rescue resources to the area where Aris was alerting.

Next, I directed Aris to the other side of the rubble pile. Because he was so large, and because his pads were toughened from training on concrete rubble, Aris mowed down the area with ease. He had no problem navigating the large, sometimes unstable, pieces of concrete. I walked a little farther to the edge and directed Aris to search the slope leading to the top of the pile. Aris was searching hard, then came back to me and barked. He really wanted me to join him to find the next victim.

But I sent him out again and as he started sniffing hard around a few boulders, I could tell he caught some scent. He paced around the area for a minute, then began barking again, indicating another victim. I walked over to him, then told the evaluator that I was calling an alert for search resources to be deployed to this immediate area.

Now I did a physical check on Aris, running my hand over his body, checking for cuts and scrapes.

This is a mandatory part of the test and I was doing everything I could this time not to fail. I did everything by the book. After I'd given Aris a close once-over, we walked off the pile and later learned we'd passed our basic certification.

I was told that Aris was the fastest dog to find any of the victims. He found the first victim in about one minute and ten seconds. He found the second victim in less than five minutes. The second-fastest dog that day needed eight minutes for its find.

I was proud of Aris and the amazing job he did that day, and also relieved that I didn't fail him. After the test, I had Mike hide for me so Aris could find him and be rewarded with a chomp on the bite sleeve.

As mentioned earlier, there are two types of certification for FEMA canine search specialists. Type 2 is the entry point, while Type 1 is an advanced standard. The advanced test included searching three different rubble piles (current testing requires just two) with one, two, three, or sometimes zero victims in each pile.

When a possible victim was found, the handler had to sketch the location on the rubble pile to help rescue teams easily find the area and start searching. Distractions such as food, clothing, and dead animals were placed among the pile, and the dogs would fail if they falsely alerted on these objects. In a real-life crisis, there could be many different odors buried along with the victims, and it would be a huge waste of time and effort if a dog alerted on something other than a human.

FEMA's description of a canine search specialist illustrates the high standards a dog and handler must meet for advanced certification:

Urban Search-and-Rescue Task Forces are supported by highly trained canines and canine handlers. All of FEMA's US&R Task Forces have canine/handler teams, all of which are trained in urban search and rescue strategies and tactics. Each canine/handler team must pass a rigorous national certification in urban search and rescue. Canine/handler teams must be recertified every three years in order to participate in search and rescue operations. The canine must be at least 18 months old to attempt the test. Most canines test after they are two years old—well-trained and physically and emotionally mature enough to do this job.

For the handler, certification includes tests regarding search strategies and tactics, mapping, search and victim markings, briefing and debriefing skills, in addition to canine handling skills.

For the disaster search canine, certification includes proper command control, agility skills, a focused bark alert to indicate a live find, and a willingness to persist to search for live victims in spite of possible extreme temperatures and animal, food and noise distractions. The canine must also be confident enough to search independently and must be able to negotiate slippery surfaces, balance wobbly objects underneath his feet and go through dark tunnels.

The team tests on two large rubble piles for an unknown number of victims, implementing all of their knowledge, skills and abilities acquired from years of training. Teams that pass are some of the most highly trained canine resources in the country. (www.fema.gov)

When the day of the test arrived, Mike, Wayne, and I were super excited, and also a bit nervous. This is what we'd been training for. This is where our dogs would shine because they loved searching and they were good at it. We each received our rotation assignments indicating which pile we would start on. We wished each other good luck, grabbed our partners, and set out for our first search.

My briefing prior to the test

The advanced test was difficult, not least because we had no way to reward the dogs between each search on the pile. The dogs were accustomed to long searches for suspects in the field, but ultimately it was up to them to maintain enough energy and enthusiasm to complete searches on all three piles.

There was a slight breeze that day, which always helps, since wind passing over a victim's location carries the person's scent. With the breeze, I walked Aris along the downwind side of the pile and let his nose do the rest. This worked on two of the three piles, helping Aris quickly acquire the victim's scent and trace it to its source.

Aris and I searched the first two piles and found two victims in each. I hoped that was the right number, because that's how many times he alerted on each of the mounds of rubble. The third pile was trickier. The victims were buried closer to the center and their scent pooled in their location, more distant from the edges. But Aris was a stud and made quick work of zeroing in on the victims' scent and alerting to their presence.

Blek and Aris passed the advanced test and earned Type 1 certification. Blitz didn't, but remained Type 2-certified, still an impressive accomplishment on any working canine's resumé.

Shortly after passing my advanced FEMA certification, I received a shirt in my mailbox at the sheriff's station. It was from my friend Chuck Williams, who was a volunteer for the department's technical rescue team, a specialized unit within the search and rescue program. Emblazoned on the shirt were the words "Search and Rescue — So Others May Live." I think it even had paw prints on it, representing a search and rescue canine handler. The motto really sums up why we go through all of the training and testing: We truly want to save lives.

Being certified as Advanced Type 1 canine search specialists was a big deal, and the Orange County Sheriff's Department began to realize the potential for the use of our dogs. The department and the Orange County Fire Authority (with help from Rob Patterson) formed a mutual aid agreement, which spelled out the use of the dogs throughout the county. This was more than I could have asked for and, to tell the truth, more than I expected.

Orange County now had three FEMA-certified canines available for urban search and rescue, and the department soon allowed us to conduct exercises during our regularly scheduled training day. The department also allowed us to attend any FEMA training required for deployment with any urban search and rescue task force. Rob Patterson's association with Orange County's Task Force 5 helped us get enrolled in the required classes, one of which was a weeklong session in Washington state that exposed the dogs to cadaver scent, among other aspects of search and rescue. This kind of training was essential for deployment with any task force and was ultimately the reason I was able to respond to New York on 9/11.

L to R: Mike Gaard and K-9 Blek, Aris and me, Wayne Byerly and K-9 Blitz

L to R: Aris and me, Wayne Byerly and K-9 Blitz, Mike Gaard and K-9 Blek,

Wayne Byerly and K-9 Blitz; Aris waits his turn

Some of the FEMA canine handlers we trained with in Washington had been deployed during the Oklahoma City bombing in 1995 and other major incidents. Some had gone overseas on international rescue missions. I was thinking, and hoping, that we'd never need to use our skills, but at least we could be prepared for "The Big One," the massive earthquake expected to hit Southern California one day.

If a large quake caused buildings to collapse, created large sinkholes, or sent trees toppling onto homes, we would be ready and know how to respond. It helps to have a plan, a trained staff, and the equipment to carry out the plan. The plan would be simple: find and save as many lives as possible.

Life went on after our certification and we went back to doing building and area searches for suspects. We continued to train on a rubble pile now and then. One day I was on patrol with Aris and received a call from my sergeant, asking me to respond to a waste disposal plant in Anaheim. He said they were requesting a FEMA dog to search a large pile of manure in which a worker had disappeared. Aris and I responded and met with other search and rescue workers at the site, but before we could deploy, the man's body was found. Tragically, he'd been buried when part of the pile collapsed below him.

This was my first experience being assigned any type of search and rescue mission. There was only one other call like this prior to 9/11, and that was a mudslide in Laguna Beach. A FEMA dog was requested to search the mud and debris that resulted from a massive slide, but another canine responded first and beat us to the punch. So, Aris and I went back to our patrol duties.

CHAPTER EIGHT

ARIS RETIRES, THEN DEPLOYS TO NEW YORK

In March 2001, I tested for an investigator position. This was why I joined the sheriff's department in the first place. My career goal was always to become an investigator. The only reason I waited so long to apply for the position was my commitment to the canine unit. I didn't plan on spending nine years of my career in the canine unit, but it was a life-changing experience that I wouldn't trade for anything.

In the sheriff's department, the investigator position is a promotion and not just a rotational position (some police departments rotate patrol officers through a detective program for a few years before returning them to patrol). In May 2001, I made the eligibility list for investigators. I was promoted quickly and joined the South County narcotics detail within the Special Investigation Bureau (SIB).

As throughout my career, Kim Markuson, the lieutenant who was instrumental in starting the canine unit in Mission Viejo, and who was by then a captain in charge of the South County division, had a part in my assignment. I remember Captain Markuson calling and asking me if I was interested in going to the narcotics detail as a new investigator. He told me that since there was already a narcotics detection dog — Jack — assigned to the detail, Aris would need to retire.

Aris was nine years old and had worked for about six years. Most police canines work anywhere from six to ten years, depending on many variables, including their age when they start. I was super excited to join the narcotics detail and work alongside some amazing and well-known investigators. As for Aris, he had more than earned his retirement and I was happy that I could keep him as our family pet.

On that dreadful day of September 11th after my 13-year-old son walked in and told me and Laura about the plane crashing into the WTC, I quickly dressed (in shorts and a t-shirt, since I was working undercover narcotics now), said goodbye to Aris, and jumped into my Ford Mustang to head into work.

While at the station, I found myself hoping for a call from FEMA and a chance to go to New York and help in any way possible. I spoke with Mike Gaard, one of the canine handlers I'd trained with for the FEMA tests, who said he'd been asked to report to March Air Force Base in Riverside County (now March Air Reserve Base) for possible deployment with the Urban Search and Rescue team from Los Angeles City Fire (LA City Task Force CA-TF 1).

Although I hadn't gotten a call, Mike told me I should go with him because they needed four dogs. I drove home and told Laura about my change of plans. She helped me grab my two red "go" bags packed with items such as helmets, backpacks, lights, and other essentials (required of every task force member in the event of deployment - see Appendix B) and load up the car.

Laura, Aris, and I followed Mike and his dog Blek to March AFB, covering the distance between counties at more than 100 miles per hour. At the base, they told us they might need just one more dog, as they'd already found three others that were qualified. I insisted that Mike should go, but being the giver that he is, he suggested we flip a coin to see who would go to New York. I called heads and the coin came up tails.

I wished Mike good luck, but he pulled me aside and said, "Look, Bob, you started this program for us. You should be the one to go."

He said more task forces would likely be responding and that he would go with Orange County Task Force 5 when called. I asked him if he was sure and he insisted that I go. I told him I hoped that he would soon be right behind me.

We waited what seemed like an eternity while all the personnel gathered (67 assigned on each task force at that time) and the paperwork was completed. A task force consisted of individuals assigned to four areas: search, rescue, technical, and medical. Our task force had four canine search specialists assigned to it.

I said goodbye to Laura and reassured her that I would be fine and would call as soon as I could. I felt bad about leaving her, our kids, and Mike behind. As night fell, equipment was loaded into the center area of the cargo plane, including many pallets of the task force's machinery and tools. The cargo also included Aris in his crate. Crating or kenneling dogs is a great way to help them relax because there's less space for the dog to be concerned about. This forces the dog to lie down and rest, and Aris would need all the rest he could get before we left.

We climbed into the Air Force C-5 transport plane and sat on the small net seats along the plane's fuselage. I began to think about all the people we would find trapped in the many voids of the collapsed buildings, and I could envision Aris alerting to a victim trapped beneath the rubble.

I thought about how I would notify the right people who could coordinate and deploy the proper rescue equipment to find survivors. I was brought back to reality as the engines fired up and we taxied toward the runway. Once airborne, I realized that no other planes were flying over the country at that moment, the result of an unprecedented grounding order from the FAA's air-traffic control chief, who, fatefully enough, had started his first day on the job on 9/11. Our flight was, in fact, being escorted by fighter jets on our journey across the country.

One of our task force leaders asked if I wanted to take a look at the flight deck, and of course I jumped at the chance. I walked to the front and onto the flight deck and my immediate thought was: "Do these kids' parents know they're flying this plane?"

These fine young men were just that: very young. But it was clear they were focused, professional, and knew exactly what they were doing. I'll still never get over how young they looked — probably because I was 41 at the time! The United States military does a fantastic job of training our young men and women with hands-on experience, developing skills that would take a civilian years to accomplish. Being able to fly this plane, during this stressful time, was a perfect example of how that training had paid off.

I returned to my seat and began speaking with one of the other canine handlers. He introduced himself as Seth Peacock, along with his canine partner Pupdog, a beautiful black Labrador mix. Seth and I would later become good friends while working the same shift rotation in New York. Seth was as eager as I was to get to Ground Zero, use the skills we had learned, and watch our dogs do what they did best: find people buried or trapped beneath the rubble.

We landed at McGuire Air Force Base in New Jersey on Wednesday, September 12th, then shuttled to neighboring Fort Dix and awaited deployment orders. We were tired and hungry from the flight across the country and had a few hours to feed ourselves and the dogs. The dogs also got a much-needed walk and bathroom break. All the dogs were kennel-trained and would not go to the bathroom inside their kennel, so they appreciated the break and took full advantage of marking their territory everywhere they could.

At 4:00 a.m., we were told to load up onto several large buses that would take us into Manhattan. This was a convoy, including our entire task force and several trucks carrying the equipment we brought.

As we drove to our destination, I looked at the high-rise buildings of Lower Manhattan and saw smoke rising high into the air. I'd never been to New York, but I'd seen many photos and movies with the Twin Towers in the background, and now the skyline did not look the way I'd pictured it. As we drove closer, it looked like several buildings were still smoking and smoldering. I realized I hadn't given much thought to *fire*, because I'd only witnessed the building collapses on television and hadn't seen any other news about the attack since then.

We arrived at the Jacob K. Javits Convention Center in Midtown Manhattan, which became our main base of operations. The convention center was already buzzing with activity from several different task forces that had arrived before us. I was impressed with how many people were already helping set up partitions to serve as walls between each individual task force.

We were told to help set up army cots that would be our beds during our 10-day deployment. I grew up tent camping and our family have been tent campers since before our kids could walk, so I was accustomed to sleeping in a group situation with a makeshift bed.

Aris made himself comfortable in his kennel, which I was allowed to keep next to my bed. He had retired from police work about six months earlier, and I knew he was excited to spend so much time with me again. In the field, we'd worked together for eight to ten hours a day, five days a week, for six years. I often spent more time with him than I did Laura and the kids.

That ended when I was promoted to investigator, but suddenly we were thrown back together, a team once again. He had a little more pep in each step and I could tell he knew that he was back on duty, eager to be back in the field. He was born a working dog and loved his job so much. Different environments did not bother him and he adjusted well to being thrown on a plane, transported across the country to an unknown city with new people all around him.

Once we'd settled in, we gathered for a task force briefing. Everyone wanted to know when we could start searching Ground Zero for victims. We were split into day and night groups with shifts of 12 hours on, 12 hours off. I was assigned to the night shift along with my new friend, Seth. This meant that our first shift would start Thursday, September 13th. We were told to get some sleep prior to our shift, but nobody was in the mood to sleep. Everyone was anxious and wanted to get started with the search.

Thursday afternoon finally arrived and half of the task force loaded up in passenger vans that would take us to our base of operations

(BOO) and, finally, the rubble pile. As we drove toward the smoke, I saw people on the street putting up posters and signs for people still missing from the day of the attack. Some were setting out candles, creating small pockets along the streets that became vigil sites for those still missing or lost in the attack. I saw people hugging and crying, some on their knees praying. It all reminded me how truly tragic this attack was.

We drove into the search area without any real security checks because it appeared that a perimeter had not yet been set up around the destruction. New York, or the United States for that matter, hadn't seen anything like this type of attack happen before. This was a terrorist attack that used our own country's commercial planes in a coordinated effort to cause as much devastation as possible. All available police and fire personnel were tied up searching for survivors and taking care of the injured. A majority of New York's Urban Search and Rescue team and leadership was in one of the towers when it collapsed. I saw several people, regular citizens, just walking up off the street and joining the rescue efforts.

Searching a huge area littered with dangers such as sharp objects, heat, and unstable footing requires knowledge and experience, and it's why we have professional teams trained for these situations. Of course we knew these people were only desperate to help and possibly find their friends and loved ones in the pile, but I worried that more people could start getting injured — or worse.

Our BOO was on the ground floor of a building on Liberty Street, directly across the street from where the two towers once stood. Here we'd stage and store our equipment and remain on standby, ready to respond to any call for assistance from the search coordinators. This would be our home away from the convention center for our 10-day deployment. The building had apartments above the ground level, which had all been evacuated.

While waiting for our search assignments, a drizzle began to fall, and the dust from the collapse was now turning into a mud-like substance. Taking my first walk on the pile, I distinctly remember the heat and smoke still rising from the rubble. Neither the heat nor smoke seemed to bother Aris.

I walked by a large trash bin spray-painted with the words "FBI Airplane Parts Only." I could see various pieces of parts lying inside the bin. Steel siding from one of the buildings was still standing, forming a sort of artistic statue. It was an eerie feeling and very surreal.

Many of the buildings surrounding the two towers were destroyed as well. I'd had no idea of the real devastation to the area, which was much greater than I had seen on television. This was square blocks of burned-out and partially collapsed buildings. Standing on the pile, I suddenly realized that I was in the middle of the largest crime scene I would ever see in my life.

Ravi Moonan pets Aris

CHAPTER NINE

FIRST GROUND ZERO SEARCH

Our first call to assist came on Thursday night, searching an area not far from our base. It felt good to finally do what we came for and I had high hopes our dogs would find survivors. It didn't take long for the first dog in our group to alert us to live scent below the rubble. I was asked for Aris to search the same area and confirm the alert before any specialists or engineers were called to start digging in the area.

Aris started his search and quickly went to the same area where the first dog alerted. He sniffed around the area and started barking — his alert for live scent — indicating that he too smelled the same odor. A third dog came and also confirmed the alerts.

These weren't extremely strong alerts, however. All the dogs barked, for example, but none of their barking was especially focused. That is, they weren't staying in one spot, barking consistently, and pinpointing the source of the live scent.

As the third dog finished his search, we were told to clear the area due to an unsafe condition. Apparently an overhead scaffolding had become precarious and unstable in the blowing wind, and it would be at least one day before we could safely resume searching. We never returned there, and later learned that some deceased victims were recovered from the area.

This was so frustrating. We'll never know if the dogs alerted to someone clinging to life, or to someone who had just passed. Unfortunately, it would be the last time any of our dogs alerted to live human scent at Ground Zero.

After our first shift, we piled back into the vans and returned to the Javits Center to get some rest. On our return, we heard that President George W. Bush would come to the convention center later that day (this was now Friday, September 14th) to personally thank first responders and also pay his respects to the victims of the attack. I was walking Aris outside of the convention center, giving him a much-needed break, when the president arrived. Aris and I walked back inside and joined a very long single-file line.

I could see the president and Senator Hillary Clinton making their way toward us and shaking everyone's hands, the president thanking everyone as he walked along. As soon as I shook his hand, a CNN reporter asked the president a question. I couldn't hear the question, but heard his response:

"They are angry at the people who caused the devastation, they are angry at those that committed the crime. Our response will be one that is justified."

It was an honor to see our president taking time to thank the personnel and also see him committed to responding to this horrific act. The opportunity came for me to use a toll-free phone, so I called Laura later that night. She told me she'd heard from many friends and family members who had seen me on the news in New York, standing behind the president wearing a full beard (my "narcotics detail" beard) and Mighty Ducks of Anaheim hockey cap. They also thought they could hear Aris barking in the background (during the visit, I was a bit concerned that Aris might get a little aggressive with President Bush; he was a police apprehension dog after all!).

Laura hadn't seen the broadcast, as she'd been busy taking care of the house and kids. Laura had to hold down the fort while I was gone, which was actually not much different from what she did every day whether I was in New York or in the field at home. Laura fixed appliances, fed the kids, handled the finances. One of my supervisors called and offered to mow our lawn while I was gone. Laura thanked him, but said she was used to doing the lawn herself.

As you can imagine, security was strict prior to the president's arrival. Security all around tightened up; we had to report to tables where our identities were double-checked, and we were issued new FEMA ID cards. We were also given a temporary World Trade Center identification card. Even Aris received a FEMA ID with his photo, which he wore proudly on his collar. These were new security measures made to ensure that only trained personnel were allowed to enter certain areas surrounding the rubble.

Every day we'd also be issued a different color sticker to place on our ID, granting us access into the now-restricted search area at Ground Zero. For our second shift of searching, our identities were checked at a new perimeter checkpoint established around the entire area to prevent people who were well-intentioned, but untrained and ill-equipped, from injuring themselves on the pile.

There was also a need to protect the first responders, as no one knew if another attack was planned on the very people trying to recover victims. There were so many unknowns at this point and the added security was a welcome measure.

As we drove to the checkpoint, I noticed more people lining the streets, holding signs thanking the first responders, and cheering us as we approached. Although I hadn't experienced a personal loss in this tragedy, I felt the pain and sadness that people were expressing on the streets around Ground Zero.

Kindness tends to follow sadness, and I saw many acts of the former. A local business on the edge of the destruction zone served food and coffee to first responders while they took breaks from the painstaking work. Seth and I walked around the convention center one day and found an area set up with donations from local businesses. It was like walking into a department store. Brand-new steel-toed boots, gloves, socks, toiletries, clothing — just about anything we needed, and all free to us. I'd never seen anything like it.

I'd worked fundraisers before and seen firsthand how difficult it could be to get businesses to donate products. But this was different. America was under attack and everyone who could donate did so without thinking twice. Everyone wanted to help in some way. I am truly grateful to those people and those business owners because their donations were very much appreciated and not taken for granted. It made our job a little easier and I'm thankful for that.

As a new search and rescue responder, I wanted to help in any way I could. And I wanted to do it now. But during the first few days on site, our task force wasn't called on very much. Not only had the citizens of New York lost many loved ones in the disaster, but also the New York Police Department, the Fire Department of the City of New York (FDNY), the Port Authority, and many other agencies suffered terrible losses. Most of the New York personnel I spoke with in the days following the attack told me they just wanted to recover their loved ones from the pile and be able to grieve their losses.

This tremendous state of shock, both logistically and bureaucratically, might help explain why we weren't called on more extensively in the early days after the attack. Our leaders continued to let the New York and FEMA search coordinators know that we stood ready, and slowly we started to work and search more often. Our dogs were eager to do what they were trained to do, but as our searches continued to find no survivors, the dogs got frustrated.

The dogs were accustomed to being successful in their searches and then enjoy a reward, so to keep them interested, Seth and I would find an abandoned ambulance or some debris, then hide for each other's dogs. I would send Aris into an area where Seth was hiding, and since Aris was an apprehension dog (the prey drive that I mentioned earlier), he would want to bite him. Seth wore a bite sleeve I'd brought and he'd give Aris a bite after Aris found him.

This was the first time that Seth had ever worn a bite sleeve and he was extremely nervous, but also very excited. Seth really wanted to support Aris and me, so he put aside his nerves, put on the bite sleeve, and hid. This is how, as a team, we worked together to ensure that we were operating at the top of our game. I'd return the favor for Pupdog, rewarding him with a toy after he found me hiding. After the first time we hid from the dogs, we let Pupdog go after the bite sleeve and, wow, was he ever excited to attack it! He took out so much aggression on it that we decided it might be better not to offer him the sleeve anymore.

The dogs loved these exercises, though, and Seth and I would hide for them any chance we could. Then when we'd get a call to assist in a search, the dogs were ready and eager to find someone and earn their reward.

When we first arrived in New York, we were issued some dust masks, and I would wear mine while searching. But I noticed a lot of the New York personnel on the pile for hours and hours without any type of breathing protection. Resting in the base of operations after completing our searches on our third day, I removed my mask and lay down on some drywall to take a quick nap. Seth came up and told me, firmly, to put it back on and wear it anytime we were at Ground Zero. He explained that everything floating in the air, or kicked up by the removal of debris, was bad to inhale. I'm forever grateful to him for convincing me to wear the mask, even though our initial ones were just dust masks.

Now we all know that many first responders who worked the pile for any length of time without breathing protection are suffering an array of respiratory problems. A 2019 study from the International *Journal of Environmental Research and Public Health* describes how WTC responders were highly exposed to the toxic substances (heavy metals, silica, asbestos fibers, and wood dust) within the settling dust cloud from the tower collapses, and how the short- and long-term effects of the exposure include asthma, chronic obstructive pulmonary disease (COPD), and lung scarring, among other respiratory ailments (see Appendix C).

I am thankful to Seth for making me wear my mask for our entire deployment. Hard to believe, 20 years later and here I am wearing a mask in public again during this horrific Covid 19 pandemic. I am wearing the mask this time not only to protect myself from harm, but also to be careful not to spread the virus to others.

CHAPTER TEN

REALITY SETTING IN

We had such high hopes when we boarded the plane in California and flew across the country, but now, several days in, the days were starting to blend together and our hopes of finding survivors was fading. We had to face the reality that this was becoming a recovery mission and no longer a search and rescue effort.

This hit home for me as I started noticing the unforgettable odor of decay in the air — cadaver scent — while working on the pile. It's an odor I first experienced as a young deputy and it's one that stays with you forever. I've often tried to forget it because it means that hope has faded, both for rescue workers and the families of the victims yet to be found.

When I looked out on the pile now, I saw that ironworkers had finished cutting and removing a mass of steel beams, and a line of people stretched from one end of the pile to the other. Each person had a bucket in hand, a "bucket brigade" of workers from nearly every responding agency. The group would remove rubble, place it in a bucket, and pass it along to the person next to them. They worked nonstop, except for moments when a bell would ring out, signaling that a body had been recovered. All work would cease until the victim was moved from the pile, then the bucket brigade would resume.

Aris and I were working alongside the brigade one day, possibly the eighth day of deployment, when he started focusing his attention on a scent in an area near some steel beams. I recognized this behavior from our FEMA training. All Type 1-certified dogs are exposed to cadaver scent during their training, and some react to the scent by wagging their tails and getting very excited. These dogs already are, or go on to become, cadaver dogs.

Others, like Aris and Pupdog, react totally differently. They will pick up an odor or scent, such as from a deceased victim, but aren't excited by it. Instead, they signal in other ways. The hair on their coats might stand up or they may urinate or defecate at the location. Their handlers need to recognize this alert and pinpoint the location of the scent as best they can.

Seth worked Pupdog over the same search area and Pupdog alerted to an area close to where Aris had alerted. Seth walked over and saw what appeared to be the boot of a firefighter sticking up through the debris. Over time and movement, the debris field was constantly changing, and what had been hidden before now became more apparent. We told an FDNY firefighter about Aris and Pupdog's alerts to the two locations and advised him to search and dig in that immediate area. The search uncovered the bodies of two FDNY firefighters who had died in the collapse. The New York rescuers who I met in the first few days had told me that everyone, except a group of survivors found in a stairwell two days after the attack, had perished in the fire or building collapses. As much as I didn't want to believe them, it was starting to look like they were right. And though it hurt that we couldn't find any survivors, I hoped we at least helped provide some closure to that firefighter's loved ones.

Seth Peacock with K-9 Pupdog

We returned to the convention center exhausted. The days were adding up and the searches weren't going as we'd hoped. We were physically exhausted, mentally exhausted, and depression was setting in. I wanted so badly to help, but found myself losing hope of finding anyone who could have survived the collapse. The amount of ignited airplane fuel burned almost everything inside the buildings. Office furniture, computers, books, files, and innocent people were all lost to either the fire, smoke from the fire, or the collapse.

As I walked on the pile, I realized that only concrete and steel had survived this horrific incident. The high hopes I'd had initially were all but gone now. Now I know why a task force is limited to a 10-day deployment; the physical demands are one thing, but the emotional strain is too great. It was hard not to become depressed as we thought of all those lost in the rubble.

Leave it to Aris to be the one to help others through tragedy, though. At one point, a couple of firefighters walked off the pile for a drink of water. These guys were covered from head to toe in dust and dirt and looked exhausted. They came up to me and asked if they could pet Aris. Once they started to pet him, I could actually see their shoulders relax and their breathing slow. Their bodies seemed to loosen and become less tense, and they appeared to, just for a moment, forget about the inescapable devastation and loss of life.

After a few minutes of petting Aris, they thanked me for helping in the searches and walked back onto the pile to continue their efforts. My spirits lifted slightly knowing that Aris and I offered relief for some first responders working so hard and pushing themselves past exhaustion, hoping to find a survivor. Aris gave these guys a much-needed break, mentally and physically, and momentarily lifted some of the weight of their worlds.

Later I understood this moment as one of the ways that Aris and I — but mostly Aris — made a difference by being there, and moments like these eased all of the other disappointments and feelings of futility.

During one of our days on the pile, our task force was accompanied by FEMA photographer Andrea Booher. Andrea was one of only two FEMA photographers (along with Michael Rieger) granted full access to Ground Zero, and her method was so unobtrusive that I didn't even notice her taking photos at first. With Andrea documenting the scene, Aris and I just continued to search whenever we were asked to clear an area. This was not the time or place for striking poses, so it wasn't until much later that I even realized she was taking them when I saw Andrea's photos of Aris, Pupdog, Seth, and me searching the rubble.

Looking at the photos brought back more detailed memories of all that was going on during our searches. I was completely focused on Aris and his searching rather than the larger picture of what others were doing around us. The search area was much larger, and quite a bit more dangerous, than I remembered. There were pits that were 20 feet deep, or deeper, so making sure Aris avoided these dangers was my first priority. The vast search area meant that our searches were broken down into smaller sections, and we wanted to make sure we covered every inch of the rubble. We would overlap our searches in order to make sure we didn't miss anything.

On our last evening in New York, the task force was invited to dinner at a fine steakhouse in Times Square by some of the local business community. These people wanted to thank us and show their appreciation for our work and effort, and the generosity of New Yorkers was unbelievable.

I was so thankful for this meal, which was quite different from what we'd been eating at the convention center. That's not a complaint, only an acknowledgment that this dinner was quite a treat, and it illustrated what I mean when I say that we all came together during this time, and how I believe that we can do it again. The steak dinner was not only a wonderful and generous gesture, but it also reflected the willingness of all those who jumped in to search and to help with whatever needed to be done. It made me believe that we need to support one another more often, and not fight or argue over the small things.

Before I left for New York, my new Dodge Durango SUV took a small rock to the side, causing a dent. When I returned home from Ground Zero, I remember looking at that dent and thinking, "I am never going to fix that dent. I do not want to fix that dent."

The dent was such a minor inconvenience and showed just how small our problems seemed now in comparison to the loss of life and amount of devastation that I'd just witnessed. I sold the Dodge several years later, that dent still on its side.

CHAPTER ELEVEN

HOMEWARD BOUND

The FAA lifted its grounding order on aircraft three days after 9/11, but air travel would never be the same again. The Transportation Security Administration (TSA) was created by President Bush to prevent a similar attack, new security measures were put in place, and people were still a little nervous about flying.

After 10 days in New York, our task force took a chartered commercial flight home. Aris was able to sit next to me, uncrated, for the five-hour-plus flight home, and I was very nervous about him flying that long without being able to relieve himself. I walked him around and got him to go several times before we took off, so I felt a little more confident that he wouldn't have an accident on the plane. He was a trained professional after all, so I convinced myself he would be OK.

During the flight, Aris, all 110 pounds of him, sat on a passenger seat next to me, or sometimes would lie at my feet. He was just happy to be out of his kennel and spending time with me. He was a great partner and I loved having him with me. It reminded me of all our time together on patrol and I missed those days. Now we were headed back, where he would once again stay at home while I went back to work.

I didn't want to think about that right then, though, so I just concentrated on appreciating our time together. The rest of the task force was tired and looking forward to home. Seth and I said goodbye and promised to get together again later in California.

Laura and the kids greeted me at March Air Force Base with a hero's welcome, complete with a "Welcome Home" banner. It was great to see them. I'd missed them all so much, and it was so awesome that they came out to the base to greet me and Aris. Little did I know that Laura and a friend had also arranged a welcome-home party for us with quite a few of our friends.

Each one thanked me for my work in New York, and while I was very thankful for these friends and their support, I still wished there was more I could have done. One friend told me they felt good knowing that Aris and I were there helping when they could not. It gave them hope and a sense of pride knowing I had trained for this type of emergency and was doing everything I could with that training to help the search efforts. I felt better knowing that, through my friends' support for me and Aris, they were in fact helping.

Another friend invited some local firefighters who arrived in one of their engines and thanked Aris and me for our service. This was an amazing gesture and a great example of how the entire country rallied and pulled together in a difficult time. Firefighters and police often keep to their own groups, and we sometimes joke about each other's chosen profession. But this was a time when that sense of division

went out the window and everyone supported everyone else under the idea that we're all Americans and we all stand proudly together.

Nearly every home and car had an American flag displayed and many fire departments started flying the flag on top of their emergency vehicles. In addition, more flag stickers started popping up on the bumpers and trunks of police vehicles. This outward display was a signal to all that we were proud of our country and all it represented, and that we stood united against evil in the world. I was proud of the way our nation came together in this difficult time.

A few days after my return, the sheriff's department asked me to participate in a press conference welcoming me and Aris back home. We were also interviewed on local news channels. This was a little tricky because I was still a narcotics investigator, and in order to be effective, you need to develop informants. Having my face on television news would seriously compromise those efforts, so for the interviews the camera view stayed below my shoulders. My friends joked that I had some very famous Vans sneakers.

The camera focused mainly on Aris, and rightfully so. After all, he was the only reason I was even in a position to respond to a search and rescue mission. Aris and his abilities allowed me to participate in one of the most memorable, and most tragic, events of my career and life. I felt an amazing appreciation for the first responders, and especially for the dogs, that responded to this tragedy, and also for all the love and support from those at home who didn't have the opportunity to respond like I did. I will never forget!

I'd never experienced any type of special recognition before my return from New York. I was just a guy who liked to surf and make beer. But after being home for a few weeks, I received offers to appear on television with Oprah Winfrey, among other hosts, or join a game show with other first responders. I was ambivalent about whether I should do this or not, and thankfully my lieutenant quickly took the decision out of my hands. If I were to appear on any of those shows, he said, I'd need to transfer out of the narcotics unit. Easy decision; I stayed in the narcotics detail.

Our deployment did catch the attention of the sheriff's department, as Aris and I were nominated for the Medal of Merit. This honor is awarded for extraordinary performance of duties that bring significant status or recognition to the department. I tried to get Mike Gaard nominated for the award as well. Even though he was never deployed to New York — CA Task Force 5 allowed another task force to go in its place — he went through all the same testing and certification that I did. He was staged and ready to go at the El Toro Marine Base in Orange County, and the only difference between us was that I had been deployed and he hadn't.

I argued that his training and readiness to respond should also qualify him for the award. Unfortunately, neither Mike nor his canine partner Blek got the recognition I felt they deserved. I felt especially guilty receiving the award because if not for Mike, I wouldn't have gone to New York and my life would have been totally different.

However, I also realized that the award was more about recognizing Aris and the canine program than it was about me. Aris and I, and my entire family, attended the award ceremony where Aris accepted his medal on stage, in front of hundreds of loyal supporters and other award winners. I was happy that this brought some much-deserved recognition to the canine unit and solidified the department's support

for the program, even allowing it to branch out into search and rescue efforts.

I continued working narcotics for several years, and each day I'd have to say goodbye to Aris and go to work without him. Luckily, I'd bred him with another Czech shepherd prior to 9/11, and on Christmas Day 2000, Aris's partner had a litter of puppies. The puppies were all black and looked just like Aris. I took my family out to where the puppies were born and told them they could have the pick of the litter. The kids were super excited because they had never had a puppy before. Aris came to us when he was three years old, and he was already trained. This would be a new adventure.

The kids picked a female pup from the litter and named her Shadow. Shadow was very energetic and gave Aris quite the run around. So while I went back to work, I felt good knowing that Aris at least had Shadow for company. Sometimes Aris would need a break, so I'd take him to a school and give an "Officer Friendly" presentation to the kids. Aris loved getting out and being around people again. His work ethic was like mine; he loved his job and enjoyed going to work every day. I could tell he missed working, but I hoped that Shadow was enough to keep him occupied while I was away.

I stayed busy after returning from New York. Aris and I fielded several requests for presentations. In May 2002, I presented my experiences of deployment at the Annual Lifeline of Emergency Medical Services conference, a gathering of about 450 nurses, physicians, social workers, law enforcement officers, paramedics, and other health care specialists. Aris and I were also featured in *The American Journal of Nursing*, which spoke about our response to the attack.

One of my favorite presentations was a slideshow at the Casa Romantica in San Clemente, California. My son Bryan handled the slides while I gave the presentation, and we found the slides were a great way to illustrate the situation in New York City after the attack. The audience at these presentations was very interested in Aris and his ability to find people buried under several feet of rubble or debris.

Many didn't know that a canine's sense of smell was so much stronger than ours.

The attendees would thank us for our service and for my first responder's point of view to the emergency response. Many had seen events unfold on TV, not only in New York, but also at the Pentagon and in Pennsylvania, and watched the rescue efforts afterward. They were thankful to understand what was going through my mind as we went through this experience.

After 9/11, FEMA Director Joe Allbaugh gave the following testimony to Congress regarding the attacks:

On September 11th, 2001 FEMA deployed 26 of our 28 national urban search and rescue teams. Twenty-one went to New York and five went to Virginia at the Pentagon site.

I visited both the Pentagon and World Trade Center shortly after the tragic events of September 11, another day that will sadly live in infamy. The devastation I witnessed was incredible and difficult to put into words. Thousands of people lost their lives due to the cruel and cunning acts of an evil perpetrated by a few. The victims of these attacks were men, women and children, people with well laid-out plans for pleasant and prosperous futures.

At these two disaster sites, I also saw the incredible courage and the dedication of firefighters, urban search and rescuers and other emergency personnel responding to the disaster. People from Vermont, Ohio, Virginia and California and many points in between came to the rescue. I witnessed the tireless efforts of men and women of FEMA working hard to coordinate the relief effort.

Although I left both the Pentagon and the World Trade Center with a heavy heart, I also left with a profound sense of gratitude for the gallant efforts of countless rescuers and volunteers who tirelessly and mostly anonymously worked in places reserved only for the Ground Zero heroes.

Three years after Aris and I returned from New York, he was diagnosed with cancer. I was in shock. This big, strong 110-pound dog was always healthy, happy, and unafraid of anything. I noticed that he'd been having trouble walking and was not eating as much as he normally did. But I also knew that his hips were in good shape, so it wasn't the normal hip dysplasia that affects German shepherds. I took him to see the sheriff department's amazing veterinarian, Dr. Bill Grant Jr., who had certified Aris's health when we first got him from the kennels.

Dr. Grant told me that Aris had cancer in his spleen that appeared to have already spread everywhere. An operation was possible, Dr. Grant said, but the likelihood of ridding Aris of the cancer, or even surviving the operation, was not good. We took Aris home and knowing that he was suffering some pain, we didn't want to delay making a decision.

I can tell you it was one of the hardest decisions I ever had to make. Do I keep Aris around because I would miss him tremendously? Or do I let him go and give him the quality of life he so deserved?

I decided it was best to spare Aris the pain he was suffering and allow him to pass away peacefully, with his dignity intact. Another veterinarian friend, Dr. Julie Ryan, told me she could come to our home and allow Aris to pass away peacefully in the comfort of his family and familiar surroundings.

Prior to Dr. Ryan's arrival, Laura and I took Aris for a short walk. Laura loved Aris as much as I did, and on that last walk together she hugged Aris and cried. I knew this would be a tough day. We fed Aris some cake, which he thoroughly enjoyed. Then I gave Julie the nod and she injected Aris with the lethal dose of drugs.

I sat there in our kitchen petting Aris and watched him peacefully go to sleep. He closed his eyes forever, and I don't think the gravity of that moment hit me until much later. I'm not really the emotional type — just ask my wife — and I hadn't yet experienced the loss of anyone so close to me. I didn't cry right away, but a few days later, I was questioning my decision and the tears came in a flood.

Everything hit me at once: the years we spent working side by side, the times we took Aris up to the mountains with my family. All of those awesome memories hit me and it was very hard to control my response. I knew I'd never have a dog like Aris again. He loved jumping into the car to go to work, knowing I'd be right there with him, doing what we both loved.

Laura was there for me and reassured me that I'd made the right decision for Aris. She'd always been there for me and this was no exception. I don't know how I would have made it through this difficult time without her support and care.

Even though Aris had passed, I continued going to schools to share my firsthand experience of 9/11 with children, most of whom were not even born before the tragedy. I would explain to them about Aris's training and just how amazing he was. Aris was trained in apprehension, narcotics, and search and rescue, and even understood two languages. He left such an impact on everyone he came in contact with and his influence led to the development of new programs within the sheriff's department.

One program allowed jail deputies to become canine handlers. They would be responsible to train and ultimately certify the dogs for FEMA Urban Search and Rescue. These deputies would work closely with the Orange County Fire Authority during any response. The department also allowed other dogs to be cross-trained in narcotics as well as apprehension. These were game-changers for canine handlers and improved the service we could provide the citizens of Orange County.

Aris's legacy lived on.

EPILOGUE

I worked for the sheriff's department for another 15 years after 9/11 and retired in 2016. In the first year of my newfound free time, I surfed nearly every day. There's something to be said about paddling out into the ocean with your friends from "surf club" and enjoying the sun and waves. I'm not the best surfer, but being in the water is so peaceful and relaxing that it becomes addictive.

Just after I retired, the wife of one of my work friends suggested that I should come work with her. She was a flight attendant for Jet-Blue Airways and explained that the airline loved hiring retired police and fire personnel. The airline's number-one value was safety, and who better embodies that than professionals who've spent their careers providing safety to the community? Not surprisingly, the emergency training received as a first responder is very similar to what the airline requires from their inflight employees.

I'd never even thought of working for an airline, but when I learned that Laura and I could fly to dozens of places around the world for free, I was all ears.

I didn't know the first thing about working on a plane or what to expect. I started reading up on the qualifications and noticed they were similar to the training I'd received with the sheriff's department. The airline required two years of customer service. Well, I'd served the citizens of Orange County for 30 years. And prior to joining the department, I was a waiter at a Mexican restaurant — the same place I met my future bride, who was working there as a cocktail waitress.

The restaurant was directly across the street from California State University, Fullerton, which Laura and I both attended at the time, and college kids filled the place every night. Serving sodas on a plane at 36,000 feet didn't seem like it would be much different from serving rowdy students in a restaurant, so I thought I had the airline's customer service requirements covered.

When JetBlue opened its next round of hiring, I filled out an application and sent it in. I was immediately rejected. Didn't even make it to the second part of the application, which was a questionnaire. Maybe this would be harder than I thought.

I learned later that I'd checked a box on the application marked "not willing to commute." This is a big no-no in the airline industry, and it's rare for crew members to be based in the same city where they reside. Eventually they might be able to transfer near their residence, but initial assignments are almost always out of state. Everyone who graduates from JetBlue's program, for example, starts in either New York or Boston.

When the application process opened again, I submitted another application, but this time indicated that I was willing to commute. I received the second-part questionnaire, submitted a video interview, then waited for a response. I was hoping that my resumé, which listed only one job in the last 30 years, would be good enough to get me hired.

I was thrilled to receive an invitation for a face-to-face interview (what JetBlue calls the "Blue Review") in nearby Long Beach, California. During the interview, I talked about the many times Aris and I worked together, and how our efforts helped and served Orange County residents. I must have done OK because I got the job.

After graduation, I was assigned to John F. Kennedy International Airport, which meant I'd be a Southern California–New York commuter for the foreseeable future. In training, I met Larry, a fellow new hire who'd worked for the New York Police Department for 20 years and had also responded on 9/11. We immediately became, and remain, friends. Since then, I've met several people within the airline who've worked for police, sheriff's, and fire departments. This would turn out to be a great job for many first responders who were looking for another way to serve the community after retirement.

The reality of being based in New York meant that I needed to live there part-time for five months, before transferring to Long Beach Airport closer to home. While living there, I had the opportunity to visit many places in Manhattan and Brooklyn. I saw the Freedom Tower for the first time and walked around the cascading pools of the 9/11 Memorial & Museum, although I decided to wait until my family could join me before stepping inside the memorial.

Working for JetBlue has given me many opportunities, including flying into and out of Boston's Logan International Airport a few times. Many people aren't aware of this, but there are two flags that fly above the jet bridges at gates B32 and C19. These honor the sacrifice of the crews and passengers aboard the ill-fated flights of Ameri-

can Airlines 11 (gate B32) and United Airlines 175 (gate C19), both
of which departed from Logan on the morning of September 11th. I
still stop for a moment every time I see them.

United later moved to another terminal and flew a flag over gate
B27 in tribute, while JetBlue took over gate C19 and continued to fly
the original flag. I have flown out of C19 as a working crew member,
and it always reminds me of such great loss, yet also reminds me to
beware of the dangers we still face and to continue to be vigilant about
protecting those aboard the aircraft.

On September 21, 2019, I was in Boston preparing to work Flight
405 from Boston to Long Beach. I was greeting customers as they
boarded the plane and because it was September, I was wearing my
9/11 ribbon on my uniform. A gentleman wearing a ball cap came
aboard and said he liked my ribbon. On his cap was a button with a
picture of a young woman with the name Lisa Frost written on it. The
gentleman, Tom Frost, who liked to be referred to as "Lisa Frost's
Dad," proceeded to tell me about his daughter who had been aboard

United 175. I recognized her name, as she lived in a neighboring city to mine in Southern California. During the flight, Mr. Frost and I had great conversations about Lisa. I told him that the gate from which he boarded this plane was the same one his daughter boarded that fateful day. I also told him about the flag that flies over the jet bridge in remembrance of his daughter and the others who lost their lives that day. It was a special time for me and for Tom, as he was able to continue to keep Lisa's name alive. Before the end of the flight, Tom gave me his button with Lisa's picture so that I might also always remember her. I have a new place in my heart for Lisa Frost and her entire family.

In 2017, JetBlue gave me the opportunity to take my entire family to New York, and with them by my side, I was finally ready to visit the 9/11 Memorial & Museum. When I registered as a first responder with the museum, my name was added to a scrolling list of first responders on display. I was humbled and grateful to be included, but as my family and I walked into the museum for the first time, we immediately experienced the familiar somber feeling of the attack. Even though it happened 16 years ago, the memory felt as instant as if it were yesterday. We went from display to display and listened to audio recordings of survivors and relatives of victims. The whole experience was amazing, but heart-wrenching.

We spent five hours inside the memorial and museum, and while walking through one of the rooms, I noticed a photo of Aris and me working on the pile. It was nice to know that he's in there, that his work was documented and will be remembered for generations to come.

Seeing how this tragic event has been preserved for posterity in New York, I decided it was time for me to record my own story, so that my children's children, and the nation, will have a better understanding of what happened that day, and a greater knowledge of the role that search and rescue canines served in the response.

The 9/11 ribbon I wore on my JetBlue uniform on the morning I met Tom Frost was given to me by the State of California under Governor Gray Davis, who presented them to all California Task Force first responders who were deployed on 9/11. The ribbon is similar to those awarded to military personnel and is to be worn on their uniforms.

Every September, I proudly wear this ribbon on my JetBlue Airways uniform to remind myself and others to never forget the tragic events of that day. I also hope it's a symbol that helps recall just how we pulled together as a nation in the aftermath. My hope is that no matter what your political views, or your race, religion, or economic status, we can remember how we came together during that tragedy, and how we can unite again to strengthen and celebrate this great nation in which we live. Our diversity and varied experiences give us our strength, and our ability to unify as a country gives us hope. God bless each and every one of you.

Photo Credits

Many of the photographs included in this book were taken by the author, Bob Wank. While the source of some photographs is unknown, all known sources are listed as follows:

Andrea Booher/FEMA News: Cover photo, pages 70, 71, 72

Jerry Manson/OCSD: Page 78, rear cover photo

Michael Goulding/The Register: Page 60 (top photo)

Robert Patterson: Pages 42, 44, 46 (bottom photo)

Seth Peacock: Page 57 (bottom photo)

Todd Schmaltz: Page 26

Many thanks to the above known and unknown photographers who captured moments in time that words could not have described, and now all can appreciate.

Appendix A

Schutzhund training standards, explained by the United Schutzhund Clubs of America:

Schutzhund is a German word meaning "protection dog." It refers to a sport that focuses on developing and evaluating those traits in dogs that make them more useful and happier companions to their owners. Schutzhund work concentrates on three parts. Many are familiar with the obedience work of the American Kennel Club's affiliates and will recognize the first two parts, tracking and obedience. The Schutzhund standards for the third part, protection work, are similar to those for dogs in police work.

While dogs of other breeds are also actively involved in the sport of Schutzhund and often follow similar criteria for breeding purposes, this breed evaluation test was developed specifically for the German Shepherd Dog. Schutzhund is intended to demonstrate the dog's intelligence and utility. As a working trial, Schutzhund measures the dog's mental stability, endurance, structural efficiencies, and ability to scent, willingness to work, courage, and trainability.

This working dog sport offers an opportunity for dog owners to train their dog and compete with each other for recognition of both the handler's ability to train and the dog's ability to perform as required. It is a sport enjoyed by persons of varied professions, who join together in a camaraderie born of their common interest in working with their dogs. Persons of all ages and conditions of life, even those with significant disabilities, enjoy Schutzhund as a sport.

Why is Schutzhund important to the future of the working breeds? A dog that performs well in Schutzhund should demonstrate a solid temperament with a foundation of intelligence and utility. He will show a high level of trainability and happiness for his tasks. These traits are highly sought after in police K9s and Search and Rescue dogs. By participating in Schutzhund, we are keeping an important genetic pool alive for the dogs which serve and protect us. It also allows owners the opportunity to enjoy an internationally recognized sport with their dogs, creating a stronger bond, and a safe, well-mannered member of society.

Source: www.germanshepherddog.com/about/schutzhund-training/

Appendix B

FEMA recommends all search and rescue task force members keep the following items ready in the event of urgent deployment:

Toiletries:

☐ Alcohol-based hand sanitizer*

☐ Toilet paper

☐ Sun block – SPF 15 or higher (if appropriate)*

☐ Insect repellent containing DEET (if appropriate)*

☐ Common medical items (aspirin, first aid items, antacids, eye drops)

☐ Prescription medication (If possible, up to 3 months' worth)

☐ Extra pair of prescription glasses, eyeglasses repair kit, and copy of prescription or contact lenses and contact lens cleaner*

☐ Comb and/or brush

☐ Toothbrush, toothpaste*, dental floss, and mouthwash*

☐ Skin moisturizer*, soap*, and shampoo*

☐ Lip balm

☐ Razor*, extra blades*, and shaving cream*

☐ Deodorant*

☐ Scissors*, nail clippers*, and tweezers*

☐ Cotton swabs

☐ Personal hygiene products

* If flying, check TSA requirements and restrictions.

Clothing:

☐ Long pants

☐ Long- and short-sleeved shirts, sweaters (to match the weather)

☐ Hat and bandana/long neckerchief

☐ Boots or sturdy shoes and extra laces

☐ Thick socks

☐ Shower shoes

☐ Jacket and rain (or snow) gear

☐ Towel (highly absorbent, travel towels if possible) and washcloth

☐ Gloves (as appropriate, for the job to be performed)

☐ DHS/FEMA clothing

Items for Daily Living:

☐ Sunglasses

☐ Waterproof watch

☐ Flashlight and spare batteries

☐ Security/money belt

☐ Cash or traveler's checks (Power is needed to make credit card payments.)

☐ Cell phone (with charger) and list of phone numbers/addresses

☐ Resealable plastic bags

☐ Three Meals Ready to Eat (MREs) or other nonperishable meals

Appendix C

Li, J; Cone, J.E; Brackbill, R.M. Giesinger, I; Yung, J; Farfel, M.R. Pulmonary Fibrosis among World Trade Center Responders. Results from the WTC Health Registry Cohort. *Int J. Environ. Res. Public Health 2019, Volume 16, issue 5.* Dust created by the collapse of the World Trade Center (WTC) towers on 9/11 included metals and toxicants that have been linked to an increased risk of pulmonary fibrosis (PF) in the literature. Little has been reported on PF among WTC responders. This report used self-reported physician diagnosis of PF with an unknown sub-type to explore the association between levels of WTC dust exposure and PF. We included 19,300 WTC responders, enrolled in the WTC Health Registry in 2003–2004, who were followed for 11 years from 2004 to 2015. Exposure was defined primarily by intensity and duration of exposure to WTC dust/debris and work on the debris pile. Stratified Cox regression was used to assess the association. We observed 73 self-reported physician-diagnosed PF cases, with a PF incidence rate of 36.7/100,000 person-years. The adjusted hazard ratio (AHR) of PF was higher in those with a medium (AHR = 2.5, 95% CI = 1.1–5.8) and very high level of exposure (AHR = 4.5, 95% CI = 2.0–10.4), compared to those with low exposure. A test for exposure—response trend was statistically significant (Ptrend = 0.004). Future research on WTC dust exposure and PF would benefit from using data from multiple WTC Health Program responder cohorts for increased statistical power and clinically confirmed cases. For full study see (https://doi.org/10.3390/ijerph16050825).

Acknowledgments

I would like to thank my entire family for all their help in making this book become a reality. Special thanks to Laura and Kelsey for their help in editing and content development, to Bryan for his technical expertise, and to Garrett for his design skills and creativity. Laura deserves a medal for her constant encouragement, which helped me stick to my writing.

This book would not have been written if not for the suggestion by my late mother-in-law, Arlene Opstad. Arlene encouraged me to write this book right when I returned home from my deployment to New York City. Without her advice and support I would not have documented any of my experiences.

I was a police officer for 30 years and wrote "just the facts" in all my police reports. My editor, Dan Frio, was a master at turning those "facts" into clear and concise sentences that helped tell the story. So, thanks Dan!

My entire experience in New York would not have been possible if not for Mike Gaard. Mike allowed me to step on that plane, placing himself at the back of the line for deployment. I am forever grateful for his ability to put others ahead of himself.

Becoming a K-9 handler was one of the best experiences of my life. I owe a big thanks to all the amazing handlers who helped train and shape Aris and me. So, thanks to Dan Downey, Elizabeth Dove, John Heppert, Jon Auer, Randy McLennan, and Wayne Byerly.

Finally, to all those that have helped along the way: Kim Markuson and Rob Patterson for their guidance throughout my career; Kenneth Zak and Lisa Wolff for their assistance during the book development process; the Napa Madness group, especially Karen Hosford, Patti MacLeith, and Jacquelyn McLean for their constant friendship and support; and all those at JetBlue that were forced to listen to my stories as they sat on a jump seat next to me, especially Kimberly Hall for suggesting that I go work with her.

About the Author

Bob Wank retired as a Sergeant with the Orange County Sheriff's Department after 30 years of service. This is his first book which was written in memory of his amazing K-9 partner, Aris. Bob wanted Aris's life of service to be shared in the hope that it would shed light on the awe-inspiring talents of working dogs and their handlers, as well as to remind people that they can put aside differences and unite to fight the evil in the world.

After retirement, Bob began a new career as a flight attendant which has taken him many places and allowed him to meet people from all different cultures and environments. It has brought him a renewed desire to reach out to as many people as possible and attempt to inject a positive attitude towards life into everyone he meets.

Other passions of his include spending time with his family, surfing, brewing beer, mountain biking, reading, and lying on the beach. He currently lives in Orange County, California.

CPSIA information can be obtained
at www.ICGtesting.com
Printed in the USA
LVHW071559251021
701465LV00001B/15